Scalping is Fun!

Part 3: How Do I Rate my Trading Results?

I0468323

Heikin Ashi Trader

Table of Contents

1. The Trading Journal as a weapon

Not many books on money management do exist, let alone for scalpers. Therefore, this book wants to close this gap and contribute to a better understanding of this particular trading style. I am convinced that precisely the money management that emphasizes the special position of the scalper in the universe of trading strategies.

In this third part of the series, "Scalping is Fun!" I want to show through the learning curve of a single trader how the trading journal, and especially the statistical analysis of this data, provides the strongest argument for scalping. Scalpers, who have a large amount of trading data, do have a clear advantage. Their data are the most reliable (most extensive), when it comes to learn quickly and effectively from mistakes and to cross the threshold to profitability. From then on, the trading journal mutates into a powerful weapon with which the scalper acts on the markets. With the wealth of data in the back, he can perform with more confidence. He grows with his data. Stable results generate confidence. Out of confidence, in turn, grow stable results.

Above all, the scalper learns to understand his own trading better. The insight that trading and scalping are probability games that he can master is growing with every single trading day. Using the example of trading results from a single scalper, I want to show how this approach can be exciting and eventually profitable. As a reader, you will experience how a beginner becomes a more self-confident trader in the course of 3 months, and how he starts to be increasingly aware of the potential of his own trading. Prepare yourself for a real financial thriller. Here we go!

2. The first 12 weeks of a new Scalper

The trading results you learn now were obtained from a female trader that I accompanied in my mentoring program for 3 months. This trader exists and is not my invention. The trading results are exactly those that she scored during her first 3 months in the stock market. I only changed her name for reasons of discretion, and referred to her in this book simply by "Jenny." Jenny allowed me to publish her results.

Jenny had little experience in trading but became aware of this possibility of making money through my first book of the series, "Scalping is Fun!" She was eager and willing to learn. We will recognize, based on her results, all the classic mistakes that traders make at the beginning of their learning curves. I am grateful to Jenny that she provided me with her data for this book. Of course, the learning curve is different for each trader. But the subsequent comments from Jenny's first 12 trading weeks perhaps make clear that the learning curve can be completed more quickly if you get seriously involved in a trading style such as scalping. It is simple: the more trades you make, the faster you gain experience.

Scalpers undergo processes for which ordinary investors sometimes need years. Jenny has performed about 1,000 trades during this period. It is clear that she thus had the chance to learn to trade quickly and effectively, and she has taken the chance. For reference, Jenny is scalping exclusively currencies. In the beginning, she was trading different currency pairs, but, gradually, she figured out that it would be better to specialize. This is also a result of a more rapid learning curve. She decided, at some point, to deal only with the EUR/USD. Of course, she did this because of the good liquidity and narrow spreads in this currency pair. She could have selected another main pair like GBP/USD or USD/JPY, but she obviously felt at ease with the euro. She chose a professional forex broker with whom she was offered a commission-based model. Unlike most other forex brokers, where the customer "only" is charged on the spread, she will pay a small commission here. At the time, this was 2.42 Euro per round turn for each mini lot ($ 10,000).

Therefore, she received excellent conditions. With the spread-based model, you easily will have a spread from 1 to 1.5 pips on the EUR/USD. With the commission-based model, this is often only 0.2 or 0.4 pip (on average). This is an enormous advantage. The euro needs only to move a little in her favor and she would already be in profit. That is exactly what is important when we are scalping.

With regard to the commissions, I reflect here again the exact amount Jenny has paid. Despite the good conditions, this was not cheap. Of course, one might object here that scalping cannot be profitable because the commissions eat up the profits. I do not dismiss lightly this objection. He is entitled. A scalper must just be good to overcome this hurdle. At the beginning, it is certainly hard to imagine that this is possible. We will see more often that, while Jenny was able to produce a small gain on a weekly basis, she had nevertheless earned no money after commissions. It was my job to get her through this period. For those who manage to make a profit after fees, scalping can be profitable. Scalpers are among the highest paid traders in the stock market.

Therefore, the accompaniment from a coach is very important in the learning phase. One can become quickly discouraged when nobody is at your side to show you the light at the end of the tunnel. I felt my job was to create the broadest possible foundation for Jenny's scalping. She would benefit from this later with increasing experience. Experience, obtained through daily actions, is what really counts. Someone once spoke of 10,000 hours as necessary, not only to learn an ability, but also to gain mastery of it.

We watch top athletes, at their top performance levels, admiringly. We listen, enchanted, to the concert pianist playing a Chopin Mazurka. The many thousands of preceding exercises we do not hear or see. The third book in the series, "Scalping is Fun!" is all about those training exercises. We will examine Jenny's progress. We will see how she tried to become a profitable scalper from week to week. We will analyze her weekly results and discuss the statistics of this data. Thus, I hope that this book provides a contribution to a deeper understanding of the unique trading style known as scalping.

Jenny had, due to her lack of experience, no rules with regard to their position sizes at the beginning. She has constantly changed them, often on the same day. Therefore, we will not involve position sizes in our deliberations, although I understand that a wise position sizes algorithm may, and should, play a role in success. For simplicity, we will act on the assumption of a traded position size of $ 10,000 for this period of 3 months. What matters is the number of pips that Jenny has realized per trade. From this data, we want to learn and work out rules for the money management of a scalper. I hope that the topic, which may seem to be "dry" or "boring," can be exciting. Last, but not least, I certainly hope that a deeper insight into this subject sharpens the view for what matters in trading and scalping.

Week 1

Figure 1: Jenny's trades, Week 1

						total
Monday	2,5	2,5	1			6
Tuesday	3,8	-7,6	4	1	1	2,2
Wedn.	-10	13	-10	18	5	19
	-25	18	10			
Thursd.	5	3	0,5	3,7	3	-2,8
	-8	-10	-10	10	-2,8	
Friday	8,4	-5	3	-4	-12	
	-9,6					-9,6
week 1						14,8

Jenny made 31 scalping trades in her first week. The figures in the table are the Pip-number, plus or minus, that she was scoring. She worked in the first week with a fixed stop loss of 10 pips. We can see this because a number of losing trades actually ended on -10. In these cases, the trades were closed by the system and not by her own initiative. This was, for example, the case with the losses of -4 or -5. However, we also see that two losing trades were larger than the fixed 10 pips, such as, on Wednesday, a loss of 25 pips and, on Friday, a loss of 12 pips. The Friday loss is due to slippage. As slippage, we consider the difference between the prices where you want to be filled and where you are actually executed. This happens with stop-loss orders more frequently than one might expect, especially since these orders are, in fact, market orders.

The scalper wants his position to be closed as soon as a certain price is reached. This is done "best" and the trader thus takes the risk of having to accept slippage. This happens often when rapid movements run against the position of the trader. Slippage is part of it and it is a sign that the scalper is acting in a real market. That means he has real counterparties with his trades. These may be banks, hedge funds, or simply other traders. However, it is usually a sign that he is not fighting against a market maker. Therefore, slippage is one of the costs of the scalping business and must be regarded as such. I had no problem with the Friday loss of -12 in my meeting with Jenny. Up for discussion was the loss of 25 pips on Wednesday. How could that happen? This was clearly not the result of slippage, but the largest trading sin of all: she moved away the stop.

Thankfully, Jenny was comprehensible. She understood immediately that this behavior would only harm her if she would make a habit of it. If she had left the stop to -10, the gains of this week would not have been 14.8 but 30 pips plus. Here you can see how negatively one such error can affect the weekly results. Nevertheless, the small gain was not that bad for a beginner. However, was it that good? Let us have a look at the statistical analysis of this first week.

Image 2: Jenny's statistics, Week 1

trading statistics	week 1
total trades	32
win	20
loss	12
break-even	0
average win	5,82
average loss	9,5
hitrate	62,50%
payoff-ratio	0,61
expectancy	0,15

At first glance, these results look good. Jenny was able to complete 20 of 31 trades at a profit. Only 11 trades ended in loss. The term for this in trading is the hit rate and was at 62.50% in the first week. Well done, you might think. However, let us look closer. How much has she won if she concludes a trade in profit? The average win was 5.82 pips. The number you get when you add all the pips gained and divide by the number of winners, namely 20. Some winners were higher than 5.82 pips some lower, but on average, her profit in that first week was 5.82 pips.

How does it look on the losing side? We see that the average loss was much higher, namely 9.5 pips. That means when Jenny loses, she loses almost twice as much as when she wins. You see: This looks a bit less glamorous. How then could she generate a net profit of 14.8 pips this week, anyway? This, of course, was due to the relatively high hit rate of 62.50%. One can reduce trading in this manner to simple mathematics. In the Friday debrief, of course, we talked about the high average loss. On the one hand, of course, the individual loss of 25 pips on Wednesday was partly responsible for the high average losses. However, not exclusively. If the average loss was 9.5 pips and stop loss stood at 10 pips, then Jenny has little tried to limit at least some of her losers. She realized this immediately, because this figure can only improve if she were able to close her losing positions quickly.

Let us have a look at the average profit. Can she improve this? Here she was lucky. She admitted candidly that she had often closed the trade at two or three pips profit, although much more would have been possible. She said clearly that she preferred to take this small profit was than having the risk that she could lose this small gain again. Understandable, of course, but this behavior violates the second part of the gold trading rule: cut your losses, and let your profits run. With this attitude, she did not let her profits run. With this destructive behavior, Jenny is not alone. I have observed it in many beginners. They are in the mistaken belief that the hit rate (i.e. the number of winners) is critical for trading success. That this is not the case, their numbers clearly show.

Jenny "saved" her hit rate for this week. After all, she had a small profit of 14.8 pips. After deduction of commissions of 113.02 euros, the net result for this week was unfortunately negative: -42.17 Euro.

Therefore, in spite of a high hit rate of 62.50 % she had 42.17 euros less on the account! Thank God, she saw this and understood that her propensity to take fast mini-profits would not lead to success. Her individual gains should therefore be bigger, and the individual losses smaller. The relationship between average win and average loss is expressed in a further number in our statistics: the **Payoff Ratio**. Goal of every trader should be to increase the Payoff Ratio, because it expresses the profitability much better than the hit rate. Here is the formula:

Payoff Ratio = (average win) / (Average loss)

We want to look at Jenny's numbers now.

Payoff Ratio Jenny: (5.82) / (9.5) = 0.61

Although Jenny only needs to make two wins to make up for a loss, but with this Payoff Ratio she would go broke slowly but surely. In the first week, she had been saved by the good hit rate, but no guarantee exists that she could repeat this from week to week. The probability tends towards zero. In other words, the work of the coming weeks and months would consist, in particular, to increase the payoff ratio. Only if this number would be stable over one, there would be a chance to become a profitable trader. Assuming the hit rate would remain above 50% of course.

Now, there is in Jenny's stats one last number: the **Expectancy**. The Trading Expectancy is the average win (or loss) the trader may expect per trade, based on its historical data. To calculate the Expectancy, we need three numbers: the hit rate, the average win, and the average loss. The formula is as follows:

Expectancy:

(Probability of Win * Average Win) - (Probability of Loss * Average Loss)

Jenny had a hit rate of 62.50% in its first week. Average profit was 5.82 pips. Average loss was 9.5 pips. We can now calculate her Expectancy:

(0.63 * 5.82) - (0.37 * 9.5) = 0.15

In other words, based on her recent results Jenny may expect an average profit of 0.15 pips per trade. If we remember that it is a commission-based model, in which she gets a spread in the EUR/USD of 0.2 to 0.4 pips, then at least here it becomes clear that Jenny does not yet have a profitable system, although her hit rate suggested this initially. Jenny did not even make the spread in the EUR/USD, and she still has not paid commissions.

After the first week, she felt clearly that a lot of work was waiting. The real significance of these numbers in all their dimensions would become clear only in the course of the coming weeks. That is what this book is all about.

Week 2

Figure 3: Jenny's Trades, Week 2

								Total
Monday	-7	5,2	2,6	2,7	-10	2,3	-1	-5,2
Tuesday	-9,3	4,7	4	3,1	1,5			4
Wedn.	3,4	1,6	0,7	5,7	5,4			16,8
Thurs.	-10	-5,7	11,4	3,6	-5,1	4,2	2,9	-17,1
	3,1	3,1	-6,2	3,1	-6,2	-8	-6	
	-8	-3	1,7	4	2,1	5,3	-3,4	
Friday	3,3	-5,3	-4,2					-6,2
week 2								-7,7

In the second week, Jenny made 41 trades, slightly more than in the first week. I was pleased to note that she sustained no major losses. As of Thursday, she decided to risk now only eight pips per trade instead of 10. We then see her emerge twice -8 in the table. This is positive because it shows that Jenny starts to work "on her defense." She begins to see that it is important to limit her losses as far as possible. That is in her case sorely needed, because on the winning side, we see again many winning trades, but the vast majority are still small. Apparently, she could not change her tendency to close the position when she had a small profit. This behavior led to the fact that she ended the week with a small loss of 7.7 pips. That is nothing dramatic, and you can call it a normal trading week, if not for the small gains. She admitted it in the weekly meeting that she was happy with a gain of one or two pips. The main thing, it was a winning trade. We hold positive that at least she kept the losses small.

Figure 4: Jenny's statistics, week 2

trading statistics	week 2
total trades	41
win	25
loss	16
break-even	0
average win	3,63
average loss	4,78
hitrate	61,00%
payoff-ratio	0,76
expectancy	0,43

We look at the data for the second week. Jenny made 41 trades. 25 of them were winners, which meant a hit rate of 61%. This differs only slightly from the previous hit rate and illustrates Jenny's need "to collect winners." We are sorry to find that the average profit in the second week dropped even apiece. It stands now at 3.63 pips. On the loss side, it looks better though. Here, the number has fallen. The average loss was 4.78 pips this time. Since the loss is still greater than the gain, the payoff-ratio is still weak of course. It is somewhat better than the week before, but with .76, it is still below one. Her strategy has thus still a low profitability. The probability to go broke is still real. However, expectancy has improved. This time she could expect 0.43 pips per trade. While that is still not much, it is clearly better than 0.2. Expressed in Euros, she realized a loss of 7.25 euros for the week. The commissions cost her 106.36 euros. This resulted in a total loss of 113.61 euros.

Week 3

Figure 5: Jenny's trades, Week 3

								total
Monday	-4,9	4,9	-5,9	-7,5	6,5	5,5	-6,2	-29,1
	-2,4	6	5,1	-8,4	4,9	-5,3	-5,1	
	5,2	-5,8	-10	-11,2	-10,2	7,3	8,4	
Tuesday	-2,4	-5,4	3,4	5,8	5,7	-0,7	3,3	49,5
	4,1	10,2	5,4	12,5	3,3	4,3		
Wedn.	5,8	4,9	3,5	4,9	4	-4	7,1	26,2
Thursd.	6,9	2,6	2,1	11,4	7,3	2,3	2,8	72,6
	9,5	1,3	4	2,5	3,7	1,9	1,9	
	-3	-1,7	4,5	-4,9	6	1,3	3,2	
	1,7	4	1,3					
Friday	2	2,1	2,5	4,5	12,5	2,6	3,5	32,2
	2,5							
week 3								151,4

Jenny was active in the third week. Especially on Thursday, as she made 24 trades. Striking are the many winners and few losers. The -11.2 Trade on Monday was again a consequence of slippage. The result, of course, with 151.4 pips was excellent. However, we have to state that the vast majority of winners remain small. She said at the briefing that she wanted to avoid above all losing trades. In other words, she played "not to lose" instead of playing to win. If it is a good week as this one, a good result can get out. In bad weeks with lower hit rates, the sum of the winners is not able to exceed the sum of the losers. Then, the weekly result is negative.

Figure 6: Jenny's statistics, Week 3

trading statistics	week 3
total trades	73
win	54
loss	19
break-even	0
average win	5,1
average loss	3,39
hitrate	73,24%
payoff-ratio	1,5
expectancy	3,27

In addition, yes, at first glance the figures are good. For the first time, the average win is well above the average loss. The payoff ratio is therefore significantly higher than one. However, this good result she achieved mainly thanks to the high hit rate of 73.24%. Here we see a clear pattern. Jenny is a person who especially does not want to lose. She prefers still a mini profit of one or two pips rather than to achieve high profits on average with the risk to have a few more losers.

I pointed out every week that she was trying to achieve her net result especially with the hit rate. Most beginners have this problem. They think high hit rate = high profit. That this behavior in the end does not produce the desired result, it was perhaps not clear yet after the third week. This criticism on my part might sound a bit harsh, considering that she had worked disciplined for two weeks and achieved a very good result with 151 pips. However, I knew from my own experience that if a trader cannot overcome a specific behavioral pattern, it leads eventually to very negative results.

In addition, she was creating many commissions with those mini-profits of one or two pips. Of course, this way she made her broker rich and happy. Expressed in euros, Jenny could earn 153.55 euros in the third week. Her commissions struck with 113.77 euros. Net result was the week thus 39.78 euros. This seems somewhat little when you consider that she earned at least 151 pips. This came from the fact that she had scalped on Monday with a position size of $ 30,000. Unfortunately, Monday was her only losing day. As of Tuesday then she scalped only with $ 10,000.

Week 4

Figure 7: Jenny's trades, Week 4

								Total
Monday	5,6	7,3						12,9
Tuesday	-1,8							-1,8
Wedn.	3,6	3	-8,4	0,9	-6,2	9,2	1,3	33,15
	-9,7	6,6	5,25	1,8	6,7	8,2	-5,4	
	6,3	-4,8	6,3	4,9	3,6			
Thursd.	3,2	-10	8,3	4,5	3,5	-11	-11,3	-30,1
	2,7	3	-12,5	6,3	16,3	3,6	0,8	
	-9,7	-10,6	-11,7	6,3	-6,4	-7,7	-4,2	
	3,8	-7,8	-7,7	4,4	3,2	2,7	4,9	
	3,9	8	3,2	3	-14,5	2,7	-3,3	
Friday	-9	-9	-8	1,8	2,66	3,3	5,8	22,66
	3,7	11	5	3,8	3	2,4	3,3	
	-5,7	8,6						
week 4								36,81

In her fourth week, Jenny made again 73 trades. However, on Monday and Tuesday she toke it at bit easy, and then step on the gas on Wednesday and Thursday. From Monday to Thursday she scalped with 10,000 $ and after the loss on Thursday on Friday only with a mini-position of $ 5000. This weighed on the net result of course.

I would call this fourth week a typical consolidation week. Each trading activity needs such weeks. The skills need to be further trained, perhaps without great results. This is also important because only after several hundred trades the scalper gradually develops confidence in his own abilities.

When he keeps his trading journal on a consistence basis, this supports his confidence and stabilizes the results.

Figure 8: Jenny's statistics, Week 4

trading statistics	week 4
total trades	73
win	49
loss	24
break-even	0
average win	4,1
average loss	5,16
hitrate	67,12%
payoff-ratio	0,79
expectancy	0,55

When I looked on Jenny's statistics for the fourth week, however, I felt confirmed my critique of the previous week. Although the hit rate was almost identical (slightly weaker) the payoff ratio does not look so good. The expectation is with 0.55 again well below one pip. Jenny can do whatever she wants. If she does not permanently manage to overcome her behavioral patterns, she will find it hard to be consistently profitable. Good weeks as the third week are then more random results but not the result of one's own ability. This the numbers testify clearly.

With the first 4 weeks and the first month over, we were able to make an initial assessment. Despite my objections, I praised Jenny, because she already could scalp well as a beginner. This style suited her obviously. She had quickly learned that it was important to limit her losses. At the time, the fixed stop was still at nine pips. This seemed to me still a little high but at the briefing, she defended this decision due to the volatility in the EUR/USD. Many candles in the 1-minute chart showed considerably more than nine pips volatility, she said. I knew this would be a point of discussion in the future, but she would continue to scalp with this stop.

She had made 234 scalp trades in her first month and earned at 205.7 pips. This is remarkable for a beginner. However, the commissions were still killing her. The net result of -137.58 euros stayed in limits. I found this very good nonetheless, because it showed that she was not far from profitability. A slightly better result in some important indicators such as the Payoff Ratio would flush money into their account. Let us not forget that in the initial phase she still scalped with very small positions. With a stop of nine pips and a position of $ 10,000, this meant that she only risked $ 9 per trade. This was just a fraction of her available capital. It was first necessary to learn and dominate the game. Larger position sizes were an issue for later.

Figure 9: Jenny's trades, Week 5

								total
Monday	-3,5	2,8							-0,7
Tuesday	2,8	8,2							11
Wedn.	-4,6	-9,4	-9,4	-4,3	3,5	1	3,1		38,5
	7,4	9,6	19,2	0,7	2,4	4,3	7,2		
	4	3,3	6,4	3,7	9,7	-20,5	1,2		
Thursd.	4,7	-1,6	2	2,4	-6,4	-7,3	-9,9		-141
	3,2	7,7	7,4	-4,1	2,8	4	-1,7		
	-41	-21	-37	-32	-17	-13	-16		
	-9	-9	5	12	3,5	8	-4,5		
	10	18	1	-1	4	-5			
Friday	4,6	10	9	2	5	-10	5,5		-9,4
	1,5	-21,5	5	-13	4	-9	4		
	9	11	2,6	-9	8	7	-19		
	-8	7	13	-18	-9	-11	3		
	-11	-10	-12	5	-9	-8	5		
	-10	-9	-8	5	7	11	11		
	6	6	-3	-3	10	1,5	8		
	-1,6	6	2	-3	-3	-9	4		
	1,5	-9	1,5	-10	-6	-5	-6		
	9	2	-3	6	17	-6	6		
	-6	1	6	1	5	5	6		
	4	4	3	1,5	-13	3,5			
week 5									-101

Jenny's fifth week showed something that happens even to many experienced traders: a relapse into old, bad habits. The human brain is a wondrous thing. Although the observer could get the impression that Jenny disciplined transposed her own targets in recent weeks, something happened in this week that actually should no longer be allowed. It did hurt. On Monday and Tuesday, Jenny did almost no scalping. Wednesday, she got a bit more active. It also promised to be a very good day, because towards the end of her trading time she was close to 60 pips! Then it happened (red arrow). Was it because she had just been scalping very well and got a bit to brave? Alternatively, had she simply a blackout? Anyway, suddenly a loss of 20.5 pips appeared. So, 11 pips more than allowed. She had at least the presence of mind to stop scalping. After all, 38.5 pips profit for the day remained. Therefore, apart from this a slip, everything seemed all right.

Thursday began with no remarkable results. After 14 trades, she had 3.2 pips profit. This is not something about which you would have to worry. Was it out of impatience, frustration, or was it the negative impact of yesterday's mishap that still reverberated? Anyway, Jenny managed to make 177 pips loss in the next seven trades. A true stunt! The biggest loss was equal the first with 41 pips. Presumably, she then tried in a kind of desperation to make up for this loss. However, these 13 trades brought little. How could they? The discipline was gone and the respect for the built up of weeks work destroyed in the shortest possible time. How could that happen?

It is a phenomenon that I know very well myself, and I know that many colleagues have to go through. One acts against reason and destroys one's own work. If Jenny had left her stops consistently at nine pips, only a loss of 63 pips would have arisen. As we can see, she had 10 losses in succession.

This statistically belongs entirely to the possibilities. My own record was 15!

Had she traded her system consistently, then we would just talk about a bad day. However, in this way she smashed her weekly earnings. Much worse was the fact that such behavior can undermine the confidence of a trader for a long time. This result is, of course, much more serious. Had she gone through this drawdown brave and disciplined, a day loss of 70 pips might have emerged. With the gains of the previous day, she stood on Thursday with -20 pips since. Who knows, with a bit of luck on Friday the week could still end up positive. Unfortunately, she tried on Friday to compensate for this negative series by overtrading. She made 83 trades, which did not help her. Those trades only produced commissions. It is also interesting to see how a seemingly harmless slip on Wednesday (red arrow) sat in motion a completely negative spiral. You can only hope that it is Friday soon and the weekend is usable to come back to your senses.

Figure 10: Jenny's statistics, Week 5

trading statistics	week 5
total trades	142
win	84
loss	58
break-even	0
average win	5,2
average loss	6,91
hitrate	66,00%
payoff-ratio	0,75
expectancy	1,08

Let us look at Jenny's statistics; we see that no reason for excitement existed. Her hit rate is stable between 60 and 70%. Only her average loss suffered greatly under this negative day. Everything would have remained within the framework, had she not changed her stops. Although the gains are still too small, she still plays as "not to lose" rather than to win, but the damage would have been limited. Needless to say that counted in euros the week of course, was bad. In addition to the high commissions of 194.35 euros 132.01, euros lost had to be counted. Overall, a negative balance of EUR 326.36.

Figure 11: Jenny's trades, Week 6

								Total
Monday	2,5	-5,2	-9,3	3,1	1,1			-7,8
Tuesday	2,4	1,8	6	-2,4	4,8	-3,9	1,3	8,9
	-1,1							
Wedn.	-8,5	-10,5	2,8	4,5	-2,6	-4,9	-1,5	9,6
	10,3	-6,5	-8,9	-5,3	4,8	6,4	5,7	
	3,5	2,6	7,1	1,7	4,7	-5,2	-8,6	
	3,2	-7,3	5,1	9,2	1,6	4,2	2	
Thursd.	-3	-8,5	4,5	4,2	1,6	-3,2	5,9	-6,7
	-20,7	3,7	3,8	2,6	2	-8,7	3,1	
	3,8	-7,9	4,6	-5,4	3,6	3,5	-7,6	
	-8,2	-7,1	-7,2	3,8	3,9	-4,3	-7,4	
	4,7	16	-3,7	8,7	-2,7	4,5	3,6	
	4,2	2,6						
Friday	5,7	2,5	5,3	2,3	-3,4	3,5	-7,5	20,3
	1,6	5,5	1,1					
	3,7							
week 6								24,3

After her poor previous week, it was of course exciting to see how Jenny would cope with this relapse. If you look at the results of the sixth week, you can see that she managed actually a kind of "back to business." The numbers were again normal, except for a slip-up on Thursday (-20.7 in red). However, this came from the fact that she had forgotten to put the stop loss. In addition, this is happens in the life of a trader. Still, the gains are too small, but at least the defensive stands again.

Figure 12: Jenny's statistics, Week 6

trading statistics	week 6
total trades	89
win	56
loss	33
break-even	0
average win	3,41
average loss	5,1
hitrate	62,92%
payoff-ratio	0,66
expectancy	0,21

The statistics show the consistency with which Jenny performs her trades, achieving a hit rate between 60 and 70%. With the average loss of 5.1, I can live very well, especially since she started this week to work with a stop loss of eight pips. I found eight pips still a lot for a scalper, but that was her decision. Since the wins are significantly lower than the losses, the payoff ratio is low for this week, as well as the expectancy. She had on Thursday a winner of 16 pips. I asked her, of course, how this had come about, and whether it would be possible to achieve more such winners. This would significantly improve her payoff ratio. At least, she made 24 pips this week, which represented a gain of 76.29

euros. Her trades caused 166.38 euros commissions. The week she concluded therefore with a loss of 90.09 euros.

Week 7

Figure 13: Jenny's trades, Week 7

								Total
Monday	-6	-6,4	11,3	-6,2	-5,7	-6,3	-7,1	⬇ -17,8
	1,9	6,7						
Tuesday	-3,6	6,9	-3,2	3,8	1,8	1,9	-3,9	⬆ 13,6
	-3,6	2,1	1,5	3,9	1,8	4,2		
Wedn.	-6,4	-3,1	-11,8	8,3	4,8	-4,3	-6	⬆ 19,1
	-1,7	-3,7	13,4	4,2	3,7	2,5	1,9	
	-6,3	4,2	7,7	4,6	-6,2	10,6	-6,4	
	5,5	3,6						
Thursd.	-3,6	-6,1	-4,6	-3,9	-4,6	-6,2	5,7	⬇ -14
	4,1	2,3	-6,7	3,7	-6,7	3,4	-6,2	
	-6,7	-7,4	-6	-6,1	-7,5	-5,6	-7,5	
	12,6	4,5	-6,3	13,3	2,5	8	15,7	
	15,4	-2,4	-4	2,5	7,4	14	-6,6	
	-6,6	2	-6,9	-6,1	4,6	4,6	-6	
	3,9							
Friday	6,6	-6,2	3,1	1,8	-6,1	-6,4	-2,7	⬆ 12,1
	8,3	6,9	6,8					
week 7								⬆ 13

In the seventh week, Jenny made 97 trades. As always, the most were on Wednesday and Thursday. I counted six trades over 10 pips. She succeeded so to realize some bigger profits. Each trader has its own difficulties. Hers was that she had fear to lose and therefore closed her positions immediately at the slightest profit. I knew she would be a profitable trader if she would be able to solve this problem.

Figure 14: Jenny's statistics, Week 7

trading statistics	week 7
total trades	97
win	50
loss	48
break-even	0
average win	5,59
average loss	5,28
hitrate	51,02%
payoff-ratio	1,05
expectancy	0,2

This positive trend was also reflected in her figures. We see that the average gain (5.59) was slightly above the average loss (5.28). In an effort to achieve greater profits, the hit rate fell as expected, to 51.02%. For me that was logical. This low hit rate must not necessarily stay, but if you invest a lot of energy in learning new thing, you often have to accept losses in another place. This explains the still weak expectancy. The payoff ratio was finally over one. She made 13 pips this week, which meant a profit of 46.00 Euro (her position sizes were between $ 15,000 and $ 30,000). After commissions (220 euros), a loss of 174.00 euros was booked.

Week 8

Figure 15: Jenny's trades, Week 8

								total
Monday	-2,2	7,4	-1,2	-3,3	-6	-3,5		⇨ -3,1
	7,2	-1,5						
Tuesday	1,9	4,4	1,7	-1,4	-6,5	2,6	1,9	⇨ -1,3
	-1,8	1,3	-3,6	-1,8				
Wedn.	-3,5	-3,1	-1,3	-2,9	-3,3	-2,3	-4,4	⬇ -38,55
	-6,3	-7,25	-6	3,5	-1,7			
Thursd.	-4,5	-4,1	-3	7	3,9	4,2	-0,5	⬆ 35,2
	7,8	2,4	-2,9	2,3	-2,8	-4,9	6,5	
	-3,5	1,7	2	3,2	2,5	6,4	5,2	
	2,1	3,4	2,2	-5,2	1,5	2,3		
Friday	-6,9	-6,1	11,6	2,5	-2,4	1,8	-6,8	⬇ -18,2
	-3,7	-8,2						
week 8								⬇ -25,95

In her eighth week, Jenny made 64 trades. At the end of the week, this resulted in a loss of nearly 26 pips, which was due again to the fact that she had barely bigger profits. The trend of the past week had not enforced. Nevertheless, something positive had to be noted. Jenny worked starting this week with a stop of only six pips. This I interpreted as a step forward and praised her for it. Let us look at what this meant for her statistics.

Figure 16: Jenny's statistics, Week 8

trading statistics	week 8
total trades	64
win	30
loss	34
break-even	0
average win	4,42
average loss	3,68
hitrate	47,00%
payoff-ratio	1,2
expectancy	0,12

Her figures show this clearly. Her average win was higher than the average loss. The Payoff ratio remained above one. Only the expectation was weak, but of course, this had to do with the weak hit rate and the still small profits.

Figure 17: Jenny trades, week 9

								Total
Monday	-5,9	1,3	1,8	1,1	-6,7	-3,5	-7,1	⇧ 3,3
	4,5	1,5	2	6,2	3,9	1,7	2,5	
Tuesday	1,5	-6,3	-7,1	2,5	-2,5	-6,8	3,4	⇩ -33,2
	-0,2	-3,6	2,5	-2,3	-4,5	-4,3	-5,5	
Wedn.	-6,6	2,2	-2,2	5,3	1	-0,1	-6,1	⇧ 17,7
	2,8	2,9	2,1	3	2,8	1,7	1,6	
	1,2	1,5	1,9	3,9	1,3	-3,4	0,9	
Thursd.	3,2	3,1	-2,6	3,3	3,6	-5	-5	⇨ -15,8
	3,8	-5	5,4	5,5	4	3,9	-5,2	
	-5,1	-5,3	5,9	0,8	-4,1	0,9	2,1	
	2,9	-2,4	-6,4	-2,4	-5,4	4,5	6	
	-4,4	3,9	2	-3	8,4	6,9	-7,3	
	1,2	1,1	2,6	-2,5	1,3	4,3	5,7	
	-5,4	-5,2	-5,3	8,9	-5,2	4,2	4	
	-0,2	-6,5	-4,4	8,1	-5,2	-6	-5,4	
	-7,6	-6,1	2,5	-6,8	7,9	1,6	-5,2	
	-6,7	4,8	3,5	-5,9	1,1	-3	2,5	
Friday	2,5	3,6	-5,5	-2,7	-5,2	3,5	1,3	⇧ 1,3
	-5,1	7,4	-5,1	2,5	5,3	-8,4	7,2	
week 9								⇩ -26,7

Jenny was obviously very motivated in her ninth week and made 133 trades. Especially on Thursday she was very active, but without success. Despite the many trades, she made a loss of 26 pips. Of course, this belongs also to the learning curve of a trader, to recognize, when you are not doing well. I do not have anything to say against 60 trades in a day as long as those trades bring profits. This was clearly not the case on Thursday. "To be busy" at the wrong time brings nothing in trading. This is reflected in the result of course.

However, she told me that she had been working on Wednesday only with a stop of five pips. "Jenny begins to see the light," I thought. If it still does not work with the profits, at least she was building a strong defense. It is the first important building block of a scalping business: Make sure that you lose as little as possible, if you lose.

Figure 18: Jenny's statistics, week 9

trading statistics	week 9
total trades	133
win	75
loss	58
break-even	0
average win	3,09
average loss	4,79
hitrate	56,00%
payoff-ratio	0,38
expectancy	-0.37

As we can see, her efforts were not yet reflected in good numbers. The expectation was even negative this week. This is a point where so many give up. She was then kinked during the meeting on Friday, and I had to do my best to convince her to keep going. Every trader has those moments and it is not self-evident that one still carries on, if nothing is visible from the own efforts yet.

Week 10

Figure 19: Jenny's trades, week 10

								Total
Monday	-2,7	-5,6	4,4	-5,1	-5,1	-5	-5,3	
	-5,4	7,7	11,1					
	-2	2						-11
Tuesday	-5,4	1	10,9					
	-5,4	1,7	1,1	5,1				9
Wedn.	-5,5	-5,1	13,6	8,7	-5,5	-5,4	4,1	
	-5,2	-4,2	-5,2	12,1	-5,9	7,1	3,3	
	3,4	1,3	-6,5	-5,2	-4,6	-7,4	9,1	
	6,3	-5	-5,5	4,3				-7
Thursd.	1,5	6,4	-2,3	5,2	-5,9	5,6	1,5	
	-5,2	12,6	9,3	5,7	-4,4	-5,6	-10,5	
	-5,4	10,6	-5,5	-6,3	-6,9	-5,8	16,1	25
	3,8	-4,8	3,7	6,2	5,3	0,5		
Friday	4,1	2,6						6
week 10								22

In the tenth week, something happened I had long hoped. Suddenly, the winners were larger. Jenny realized multiple winners over 10 pips namely on four of 5 days! Her stop was still on five pips, but the numbers showed clearly that something changed. She stayed with her winners longer and did not close them immediately, as soon as she had one or two pips profit. Of course, I praised her for this success, which she also clearly enjoyed. It did not look this way in the previous weeks that this would still be possible, but she had actually done it! Although the week profit with 22 pips was still modest, I was sure that we would soon see winners of 20 pips and more. This then of course makes a whole difference, if she would continue to limit her losers in a disciplined way.

Figure 20: Jenny's statistics, Week 10

trading statistics	week 10
total trades	73
win	37
loss	36
break-even	0
average win	4,69
average loss	4,02
hitrate	50,68%
payoff-ratio	1,16
expectancy	0,33

Jenny made 73 trades this week. The average profit was again higher than the average loss, which significantly improved her payoff ratio. Only the expectation was a little skinny, but I was sure that it would also change soon. How this sudden improvement came about now? Ultimately, it was a small measure of which I had advised her the week before. She had told me that she put the stop to breakeven as soon as the position was a few pips in profit. I did not know this before the ninth week and asked her not to do so from the tenth week. The result of this action was reflected immediately in better numbers. Such things are happening more often in a learning curve. In principle, the trader understands relatively quickly what is important. One need not be a mathematical genius to truly understand the relationship between these simple statistical ratios. Yet sometimes it depends on small changes in trading behavior, which ultimately make the difference between profit and loss. I had, therefore, according to this tenth week the feeling that she had achieved a breakthrough, especially since the change involved into her basic pattern: namely, always to play for safety. Jenny had started playing to win.

Week 11

Figure 21: Jenny's trades, week 11

								Total
Monday	-5	8,5	-2	-5,2	2,1	3,6	-5	
	2,2	-5,2						-6
Tuesday	-5	2,7	2,3	-1,1	-0,4	-0	8,5	
	1,9	-5,3	2,1	5,6	-5,6	2,7		8
Wedn.	8,1	-4,3	3,6	1,9				9
Thursd.	2,7	4,5	24,5	3,9	10,2	1,7	-5,6	
	4,2	-5,1	-4,9	-5	10,3	-5		36
Friday	5,5	-5	-5,7	-6	-4,7	-5	7,1	
	-5,1	3,8	3,6					-11
week 11								36

Jenny made 49 trades in the eleventh week. Big surprise! On Thursday, it happened finally: Jenny closed a trade with a profit of 24.5 pips! We had often talked about this that if she succeeded, from time to time, to achieve a greater profit, this precisely would make all the difference. That one win was responsible for 68% of her weekly gains. It may not always be the case that big winners have such a weight. One can safely achieve profits of 10 or 12 pips as good results. Nevertheless, I am of the opinion that an occasional "Jackpot" increases the results considerably, not to mention the confidence gained by such trades.

Added to this was her understanding that it is often sufficient to scalp just 2 hours a day. Too often, she had experienced that more hours do not necessarily mean more profit, but certainly more commissions to the broker. Exceptions exist, especially if the scalper has the feeling that the market is very good, and that much more is to come. In this case, I recommend even to increase the position size whereas I reduce on weak days the position size or I simply finish scalping early. The control of the position size is a very important parameter that does not have a place in this third part of the series "Scalping is Fun!" I did not take in the book because it would complicate the figures and its evaluation unnecessary.

Figure 22: Jenny's statistics, Week 11

trading statistics	week 11
total trades	49
win	26
loss	23
break-even	0
average win	5,23
average loss	3,41
hitrate	53,06%
payoff-ratio	1,53
expectancy	1,17

Let us look at Jenny's statistics for the eleventh week; we note that the good trend of the week was confirmed. Now, the figures are interesting. The average win of 5.23 is well above the average loss of 3.41. The payoff ratio of 1.53 is now very good. In addition, Jenny can count on at least 1.17 pip per Trade, which is already a good number for a scalper. The hit rate has suffered a bit, but I was confident that it would rise again with increasing experience. Jenny made this week a 54.77-euro profit. The sum of her commissions was 76.32 euros. Thus, the net weekly income was -21.54 Euro. In other words, Jenny was getting close to cross the profitability threshold. Let us not forget that she was still scalping very small lots on the forex. However, she was so reasonable, not to increase the lot size as long as she was not profitable scalping after fees.

Week 12

Figure 23: Jenny's trades, week 12

							Total
Monday	5	4,1	6,4	-5	1,8	4	23
	7						
Tuesday	-5,1	3	-5	-5	-5,8		
	-5,7	-5,1	2,5	-5,1	6,9	8,7	
	2,5	-1,3	2,9	3,2	-5		-13
Wedn.	-5,1	4,2	-5	5,5	3,7	-3,2	0
Thursd.	4	6,6	-5,1	-4,2	7,9	1,8	
	16,1	5,2	5,5				32
Friday	5,5	4					9
week 12							51

In the twelfth week we see further confirmation that Jenny is well on her way to become a good scalper. Her results are now stable the third week in a row. She is disciplined and limits her losses consistently to five pips. Occasionally she has also a bigger winner, which increases her week result.

Figure 24: Jenny's statistics, Week 12

trading statistics	week 12
total trades	39
win	24
loss	15
break-even	0
average win	4,39
average loss	2,37
hitrate	61,00%
payoff-ratio	1,85
expectancy	1,78

The statistical ratios confirmed my positive impression. The average profit is now almost twice as high as the average loss. Through a time stop we had introduced a week before, she was able to reduce her losses, which of course came too good for the Payoff- Ratio. In addition, the expectation is now approaching almost two pips, which is great for a scalper.

Jenny earned this week after fee 29.80 Euro. This may not seem much, but she finally arrived into profitability. Moreover, this profitability is not on shaky ground, as was the case in the third week, when she tried it using the hit rate. She now makes money, because she keeps her losers as small as possible and she maximize her winners.

3. How is Jenny doing now?

You know now the results of the first 1000 trades that Jenny has done. These figures are more than one year old. Jenny has become a profitable scalper who trades with multiple standard lots in the forex market and makes a living of on her scalping business. Her Payoff Ratio has stabilized in the range 1.50 to 1.90 and her hit rate is still between 55 and 60%. Of course, she pays now even more fees, but she could negotiate better terms with her broker, due to high volume of her trading. I had advised her to do so.

Nothing is set in stone and everything is negotiable in this world. Whoever is a good customer, as all scalpers are, can present himself confidently and negotiate terms. This of course of high importance when commissions are sometimes in the thousands, as is the case with very active scalper. Nevertheless, you should weigh also here the amount of fees to the quality of the broker. Favorable conditions are of no use if you get spreads that are worse and when the slippage is rampant. So, talk to your broker. It is worth mostly.

4. Scalping is a Business

I hope to have demonstrated with this exemplary case that scalping is not some gimmick, but a real business. This means that one must overcome real costs, such as commissions and spreads. Moreover, there is always slippage. As a scalper, you do not get always the desired price, even if there is a hard stop in the market.

Trading and Scalping are hard and only the best survive. Whoever denies this, does not know what it is. However, I wanted to show with the learning curve of Jenny's first 3 months that it is possible to learn this business. With well-placed foundations, it can be very profitable. You know: in the stock market, no limits exist on the upside. First, every trader must master the hard lessons. Those who have learned the craft properly, have a definite chance in this business.

I wish you success!

Heikin Ashi Trader

Scalping Is Fun!

Part 4: Trading Is Flow Business

Trading profits are not equal on the 20 trading days of each month as a regular office job probably would. Experience shows that the results are asymmetrical in occurrence.

There are days where it runs like clockwork and days on which trading seems to produce only losses. In this fourth installment of the series "Scalping Is Fun!" The Heikin Ashi Trader looks at the right time to trade.

Successful traders know in specifics when not to trade. They focus on the times when market conditions are optimal for them. In order of events, the fun turns by itself, then the success follows suit.

In this state of "flow" discipline, this is easy to achieve. Fast scalping promotes the rapid close of loss positions and the quick takeaway from accrued profits, also of equal importance.

Index

How to start a Trading Business with $500

Many new traders have little capital available in the beginning, but this is not an obstacle to starting a trading career anyway.

However, this book is not about how to grow a $500 account into a $500,000 account. It is precisely these exaggerated return expectations that bring most beginners to failure.

Instead, the author shows, in a realistic way, how you can become a full-time trader in spite of limited start-up capital. This applies both for traders who want to remain private, as well as for those who want to eventually trade customer funds.

This book shows step by step how to do it. In addition, there is a concrete action plan for each step. Anyone can be a trader in principle, if he or she is willing to learn how this business works.

Contents

About the Author

Heikin Ashi Trader is recognized worldwide as the specialist in scalping with the Heikin Ashi chart. He has been trading this way for 19 years. He traded for a hedge fund and then went into business for himself as a trader. His scalping book "Scalping is Fun!" is an international bestseller and has been sold more than 30,000 times. You can find more information about his scalping method on his website www.heikinashitrader.net

Imprint

Texts: © Copyright by Heikin Ashi Trader

Swiss Post Box 106287

Zürcher Strasse 161

CH-8010 Zürich

Switzerland

www.ingramcontent.com/pod-product-compliance
Lightning Source LLC
Chambersburg PA
CBHW070413190526
45169CB00003B/1236